GEARHEAD
GARAGE

Gearhead Garage

INDY CARS

PETER BODENSTEINER

BLACK
RABBIT
BOOKS

Bolt is published by Black Rabbit Books
P.O. Box 3263, Mankato, Minnesota, 56002.
www.blackrabbitbooks.com
Copyright © 2017 Black Rabbit Books

Design and Production by Michael Sellner
Photo Research by Rhonda Milbrett

Library of Congress Control Number: 2015954923

HC ISBN: 978-1-68072-031-0   PB ISBN: 978-1-68072-260-4

Printed in the United States at CG Book Printers,
North Mankato, Minnesota, 56003. PO #1790 4/16

Web addresses included in this book were working and appropriate at the time of publication. The publisher is not responsible for broken or changed links.

CONTENTS

CHAPTER 1

Fast Racers

The green flag flies. The Indianapolis 500 roars to a start. Thirty-three cars race down the track. Cars **slingshot** through the first turn. Then they pick up speed in the straight spots. Each driver hopes his or her car is the fastest.

COCKPIT

FRONT WING

ROLL HOOP

REAR WING

FUEL "BULL'S EYE"

Racing Almost Anywhere

The Indy 500 is the most famous Indy car race. Cars there race around an oval track. But these quick cars race on many tracks. Some races are road courses. Other races are on tight city streets. Indy cars are built to reach high speeds on any course.

Indy cars look similar to Formula 1 cars. But Indy cars are larger and tougher.

The Indianapolis Motor Speedway (IMS) is the home of Indy car racing. The Indy 500 is held there.

One lap is
2.5 miles
(4 kilometers)

First race was held in 1911.

A race is 200 laps

stadium seats 257,325 fans

CHAPTER 2

The History of Indy Cars

Indy car history begins at the IMS. In the early 1900s, U.S. car racing was just beginning. Drivers raced on horse tracks. In 1909, builders began working on a track for cars. The track's owners planned to race new cars there. Then fans would want to buy them.

Going Faster and Faster

Over time, the Indy 500 became very popular. Teams began building cars just for that race. Early Indy cars had **engines** in the front.

Then in the 1960s, teams put engines in the back. These cars were even faster. In the 1970s, teams added **wings** to their cars. Wings helped cars push through the air.

When racing, the tires get so hot they melt a little. That melting makes the tires sticky.

Safety Features

Cars pushed to speeds of 200 miles (322 km) per hour in the early 1970s. Safety features became more important. Teams built cars that broke apart in crashes. This design protected drivers.

Over time, racing speeds rose too high. Racing wasn't safe. Indy 500 officials created rules. All teams must follow them. Today, Indy cars are almost all the same. Teams make small changes to be the fastest.

INDY 500
FASTEST QUALIFYING SPEEDS

Indy 500 racers run laps on the track before each race. A racer's average lap speed is called a qualifying speed. The racer with the fastest speed starts at the front of the race.

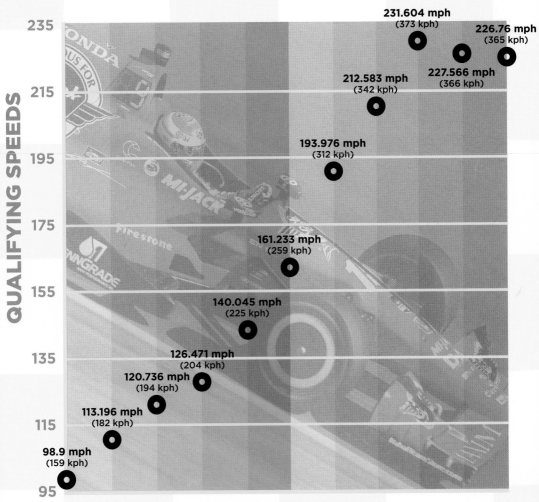

QUALIFYING SPEEDS

231.604 mph	(373 kph)
226.76 mph	(365 kph)
227.566 mph	(366 kph)
212.583 mph	(342 kph)
193.976 mph	(312 kph)
161.233 mph	(259 kph)
140.045 mph	(225 kph)
126.471 mph	(204 kph)
120.736 mph	(194 kph)
113.196 mph	(182 kph)
98.9 mph	(159 kph)

235
215
195
175
155
135
115
95

1915 1925 1935 1946 1955 1965 1975 1985 1995 2005 2015

DRIVERS

Indy car drivers come from all over the world.

JAMES HINCHCLIFFE
(CANADA)

MARCO ANDRETTI
(UNITED STATES)

RYAN HUNTER-REAY
(UNITED STATES)

JUAN PABLO MONTOYA
(COLOMBIA)

HELIO CASTRONEVES
(BRAZIL)

TAKUMA SATO
(JAPAN)

JAMES JAKES
(UNITED KINGDOM)

SEBASTIEN BOURDAIS
(FRANCE)

ORIOL SERVIA
(SPAIN)

WILL POWER
(AUSTRALIA)

CHAPTER 3

Wings, Wheels, and Wind

Indy cars are light and fast. They also have open wheels and open cockpits. **Turbocharged** engines push them around tracks. An Indy car goes from 0 to 100 miles (161 km) per hour in three seconds.

248 POUNDS (112 kilograms)

weight of an Indy car's twin-turbo V-6 engine

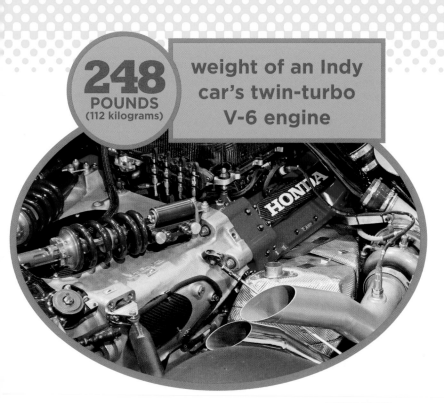

Wings

help the cars grip the track.

Wide tires stick to the road.

Quick Pit Stops

Indy cars hold just 18.5 gallons (70 liters) of fuel. The cars stop during races for more fuel. As they fill up, crews also change tires. Crews lift the cars with air jacks. One nut holds each wheel. Crew members race to unscrew the nuts. Then they replace the wheels and screw them back in place.

235
miles (378 km)
per hour
TOP SPEED

Indy Cars By the Numbers

weight
1,575 pounds
(714 kg)

height
40 inches
(102 centimeters)

maximum width
78.5 inches
(199 cm)

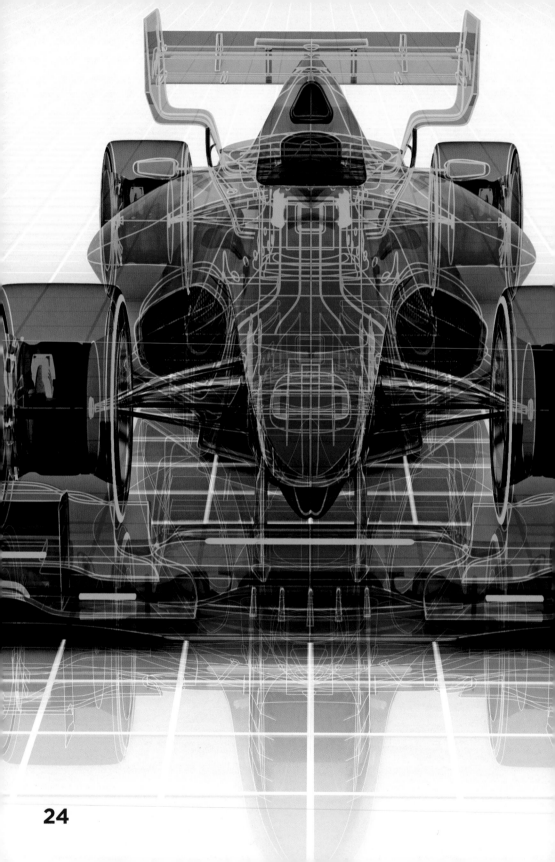

CHAPTER 4

The  of Indy Cars

Today, Indy cars race across the United States and Canada. Fans want to see faster, more exciting races. Teams are always trying to improve their cars. New technology, such as 3D printing, might help teams in the future.

Always Improving

Teams continue to make Indy cars faster and safer. No one knows the future of Indy cars. But they are sure to be fun cars to watch.

Drivers, to your cars!

1911

First Indy
500 race.

1942–1945

No Indy
500 races
run while
the United
States fights
in World
War II.

1900

United
States enters
World War I.

1917

World War II
ends.

1945

The first
people
walk on
the moon.

1969

1956

Engine changes give cars the roar that's known today.

1972

First wing is used.

2002

SAFER barrier installed at IMS.

2005

Terrorists attack the World Trade Center and Pentagon.

2001

cockpit (KOK-pit)—the area in a boat, plane, or car where a driver sits

engine (EN-jin)—a machine that changes energy into mechanical motion

qualifying (KWAL-uh-fy-ing)—the timed laps drivers run before a race to earn a starting spot in the race

SAFER barrier (SAYF-ur BAYR-ee-uhr)—a wall around a racetrack that helps prevent injures during crashes

slingshot (SLING-shaht)—a move in auto racing when a car speeds past another car

turbocharged (TUR-bo-charjd)—having a device that increases an engine's power

wing (WING)—a part of a race car that sticks up to allow air to push down on it

BOOKS

Mason, Paul. *Indy Cars.* Motorsports. Mankato, MN: Amicus, 2011.

Riggs, Kate. *Indy Cars.* Seedlings. Mankato, MN: Creative Education, 2014.

Von Finn, Denny. *Indy Cars.* The World's Fastest. Minneapolis: Bellwether Media, 2011.

WEBSITES

Fun Facts about IndyCars
a.espncdn.com/rpm/irl/2003/0520/1556796.html

Indy 500 Traditions and FAQs
www.indianapolismotorspeedway.com/events/ indy500/history/indy-500-traditions-faqs/faqs

The Official Site of IndyCar News, Drivers, Schedule, & Shop
www.indycar.com

INDEX